M4 MAC MINI REVIEW
Design, Power, and Performance - Everything You Need to Know

*How Apple's Affordable Desktop Is
Redefining Computing*

J. Andy Peters

Table of Contents

Introduction

The evolution of computing has always been marked by a drive toward making devices smaller, more efficient, and increasingly powerful. Apple, a pioneer in shaping the tech landscape, has long embraced this challenge. Among its innovations, the Mac Mini stands out as a significant milestone—a compact yet capable desktop computer that has evolved over the years to meet the demands of a changing world.

Introduced in 2005, the Mac Mini was Apple's answer to a growing desire for affordable entry points into the Mac ecosystem. It offered users the versatility of MacOS without the expense of an iMac or the portability of a MacBook. Over time, the Mac Mini became a staple for budget-conscious users, developers, and those needing a reliable machine in a small form factor. Yet, while its role in Apple's product lineup was important, it rarely received the spotlight. For many years, the Mac Mini quietly played its part as the unsung hero of Apple's desktop range.

The M4 Mac Mini, however, changes everything. Unlike its predecessors, this version has not only embraced but also redefined compact computing. Apple's decision to shift to its own silicon marked a turning point, and the M4 chip represents the latest leap in that journey. Packing remarkable performance into an even smaller design, the M4 Mac Mini is a triumph of engineering and innovation. It isn't just another iteration; it's a complete reimagining of what a desktop can be. This device reflects Apple's vision for the future: powerful, efficient, and elegantly simple.

This book aims to dive deep into this remarkable device, peeling back the layers to understand why it's such a pivotal moment for the Mac Mini. From its design, which challenges the boundaries of compact computing, to its performance, which rivals larger and more expensive desktops, the M4 Mac Mini offers an unprecedented balance of value and power. By exploring its features and significance in detail, this book provides an insider look at Apple's latest innovation and why it matters in the broader tech landscape.

Whether you're a long-time Mac user, a tech enthusiast, or someone considering their first foray into the Apple ecosystem, this book offers everything you need to know about the M4 Mac Mini. Together, we'll uncover what makes this tiny powerhouse stand out and how it's reshaping our expectations of what a desktop computer can be.

Chapter 1: The Unveiling of the M4 Mac Mini

Apple has always been known for its meticulously crafted product launches, often accompanied by high-profile events that showcase the latest innovations to the world. These events have become part of the brand's identity, with millions tuning in to watch sleek presentations that blend technology and theater. However, for the launch of the M4 Mac Mini and its accompanying updates to the Mac lineup, Apple took a strikingly different approach, opting for a series of press releases instead of a grand stage event.

This decision was both surprising and strategic. By forgoing a traditional launch event, Apple shifted its focus from spectacle to substance, letting the products speak for themselves. Over the course of a week in late October, Apple unveiled updates to its Mac lineup, including the highly anticipated M4 Mac Mini, through carefully timed announcements. Each press release was concise yet impactful, emphasizing the practical advancements and innovations that these products brought to the table.

For the M4 Mac Mini, this approach felt particularly fitting. The Mac Mini has never been the most glamorous item in Apple's portfolio—it's a workhorse, celebrated for its utility rather than its flash. Highlighting its significance through a press release allowed Apple to position it as an accessible, no-frills solution that packs extraordinary power into a tiny frame. It underscored the product's practicality and affordability while appealing to both new and loyal Mac users.

Apple's decision to avoid a major event also hinted at a shift in how the company communicates its updates. It was a nod to the evolving expectations of its audience—consumers who are now more informed and less reliant on elaborate presentations to gauge a product's worth. The press release strategy aligned perfectly with the straightforward, functional appeal of the M4 Mac

Mini, demonstrating Apple's ability to adapt its messaging to suit the moment.

This unconventional launch highlighted a growing trend in the tech industry: focusing on the substance of what's being introduced rather than the spectacle of how it's unveiled. For Apple, it marked a subtle yet deliberate recalibration, signaling confidence in the strength of its products to capture attention without the need for an elaborate stage. The M4 Mac Mini, as one of the stars of these announcements, epitomized this philosophy—quietly revolutionary, much like its debut.

The first glimpse of the M4 Mac Mini leaves an immediate impression: it's remarkably small, even by the standards set by its predecessors. Apple's latest iteration takes compact computing to new extremes, presenting a desktop so diminutive it almost defies expectations. Measuring just five inches by five inches and standing a mere two inches tall, this tiny powerhouse feels more like a conceptual prototype than a fully functional desktop. Yet, it's very real and remarkably capable.

Visually, the M4 Mac Mini retains some of the familiar design cues of its lineage but with a clear evolution. While earlier versions embraced a simple, utilitarian aesthetic, this update leans into modern minimalism with sharper edges and a refined profile. It feels less like a direct successor to the older Mac Mini and more like a scaled-down version of the Mac Studio, Apple's premium compact desktop. This shift subtly repositions the Mac Mini, giving it a sleeker and more contemporary presence on any workspace.

When compared side by side with the older Mac Mini, the differences are striking. The previous models, though compact in their own right, now appear comparatively bulky. The reduced footprint of the M4 version is a testament to Apple's commitment to pushing the boundaries of what's possible in terms of size and efficiency. The new design feels deliberate, reflecting not just advancements in hardware but also a clear vision of how desktop computing is evolving in an era where portability and space-saving solutions are increasingly valued.

The parallels to the Mac Studio are equally noteworthy. While the Mac Studio commands attention with its larger size and bold, professional-grade stance, the M4 Mac Mini feels like its understated sibling—a quieter, more unassuming counterpart that sacrifices none of the elegance. The new Mini's design choices, from its precision-milled aluminum casing to its carefully arranged ports, echo the Mac Studio's attention to detail, albeit on a smaller scale.

This unexpected compactness is more than just an aesthetic triumph; it redefines the expectations for what a desktop computer can look like. Apple's ability to condense so much power into a frame smaller than a roll of duct tape feels almost absurd. Yet, it's a reminder of the company's dedication to innovation, where even the most practical designs are infused with a sense of wonder. The M4 Mac Mini may be tiny, but it commands attention, making it clear from the first impression that this is no ordinary desktop computer.

Chapter 2: Redefining Compact Design

The M4 Mac Mini's dimensions are nothing short of astonishing. Measuring just five inches by five inches with a height of two inches, its compactness redefines what it means to have a desktop computer. It's hard to overstate how much of a leap this is in terms of design, particularly for a machine capable of the performance it delivers. The form factor isn't just small—it's shockingly small, leaving those who first encounter it questioning how so much functionality can fit into such a tiny frame.

To put its size into perspective, the M4 Mac Mini's footprint is smaller than the base of most standard desktop monitors. It's dwarfed by a typical mini ITX build, which has long been regarded as the gold standard for compact computing. While mini ITX systems often require custom cases and careful planning to achieve their size, Apple's M4 Mac Mini takes the concept a step further, integrating powerful hardware into a form factor that feels impossibly efficient. This achievement becomes even more impressive considering the device is ready to go out of the box, with no need for additional assembly or optimization.

The comparisons don't end with other desktops. The Mac Mini is now smaller than many household items, offering a striking contrast to its powerful capabilities. It's smaller than a camera body with a lens attached, smaller than a new roll of duct tape, and only slightly larger than the Apple TV. These comparisons highlight the absurdity of its size—a playful yet deliberate testament to Apple's engineering prowess. It's not just small; it's almost comically tiny for what it delivers.

This relentless pursuit of minimalism isn't new for Apple. The company has a history of pushing the boundaries of design, striving to make its devices as compact and portable as possible. The M4 Mac Mini feels like the culmination of this effort, a product that takes Apple's obsession with efficiency to its logical extreme. Unlike other compact devices that might sacrifice functionality for size, the M4

Mac Mini strikes a delicate balance, offering an array of ports, an efficient cooling system, and unparalleled performance for its category—all without compromising its dimensions.

In a world where compactness is often associated with compromise, the M4 Mac Mini challenges the norm. It redefines the expectations for what a desktop computer can look like, proving that great things truly can come in small packages. This tiny machine isn't just a technological marvel—it's a bold statement about the future of computing.

Apple's journey toward creating compact yet powerful devices has been a defining characteristic of the company's design philosophy. From the earliest days of the Macintosh to the latest innovations in the M4 Mac Mini, Apple has consistently sought to deliver machines that balance form and function without compromise. This obsession with smallness isn't a mere design choice; it's a reflection of Apple's commitment to creating technology that integrates seamlessly into users' lives, offering high performance in an unobtrusive footprint.

Over the years, Apple has pushed the boundaries of what's possible with compact devices. The MacBook Air was a game-changer when it debuted as one of the thinnest laptops ever made, and the "trashcan" Mac Pro, though controversial, represented an audacious attempt to combine workstation-class power with an unprecedentedly small design. The M4 Mac Mini is a natural extension of this philosophy, building on Apple's legacy while leveraging the efficiency of Apple silicon to achieve what seemed impossible: a desktop so small it almost redefines the category.

One of the most striking aspects of the M4 Mac Mini's design is its port layout, which manages to provide a surprising amount of connectivity despite the limited space. The back of the device features a full-size HDMI port, Gigabit Ethernet, and three Thunderbolt ports, catering to professionals and casual users alike. The inclusion of two USB-C 3 ports on the front adds convenience, allowing users to quickly connect peripherals without reaching behind the machine. Even the classic headphone jack finds a place in this tightly packed configuration.

However, the absence of USB-A ports signals a decisive shift. While Apple has been phasing out this older standard across its devices, its omission here highlights the company's confidence in the adoption of USB-C and Thunderbolt. For some users, this change may require the use of adapters or new cables, but it aligns with Apple's forward-looking approach, encouraging users to embrace the latest technologies.

One design choice that has sparked significant conversation is the placement of the power button. Located at the bottom back corner of the device, it's a decision that feels intentionally quirky, perhaps even provocative. It's not immediately accessible and requires the user to tilt or lift the device to locate it. While this placement may seem baffling at first, it's unlikely to be a major inconvenience in everyday use. After all, most users rarely turn their desktop computers off completely, relying instead on sleep modes or other methods of power management. Still, the button's location has become a talking point, fueling speculation about whether Apple made this choice to generate buzz or simply as a result of its unconventional design constraints.

The M4 Mac Mini embodies Apple's relentless pursuit of minimalism, reflecting the company's ability to combine aesthetics with engineering. Every design decision, from the port arrangement to the controversial power button placement, underscores Apple's desire to make its devices both functional and uniquely distinctive. This obsession with smallness is not just about shrinking dimensions; it's about reimagining what technology can be, challenging conventions and setting new standards for the future of computing.

Chapter 3: Power Meets Portability

The introduction of the M4 chip marks a significant milestone in Apple's quest to merge power with efficiency. This latest addition to Apple's custom silicon lineup elevates the performance of the Mac Mini to unprecedented levels, redefining what users can expect from a compact desktop computer.

At the heart of the M4 chip lies a meticulously engineered architecture that enhances both speed and energy efficiency. Building on the success of its predecessors, the M1 and M2 chips, the M4 introduces a 10-core CPU and a 10-core GPU in its base configuration. This setup doubles the unified memory to 16GB, allowing for smoother multitasking and more robust handling of demanding applications. The integration of these components into a single system-on-a-chip (SoC) design streamlines communication between the CPU, GPU, and neural engine, reducing latency and boosting overall performance.

When the M1 chip was introduced, it marked Apple's bold departure from Intel processors, showcasing impressive gains in speed and efficiency with its 8-core CPU and up to an 8-core GPU. The M2 chip continued this trajectory, offering enhanced processing power and graphics capabilities. However, the M4 chip takes these advancements even further, delivering a level of performance that surpasses not only previous Apple silicon but also many competing desktop processors on the market.

One of the standout features of the M4 chip is its exceptional single-core performance. This means that everyday tasks feel noticeably faster—applications launch swiftly, web pages load promptly, and the overall user experience is remarkably smooth. This efficiency doesn't just make routine computing more pleasant; it also benefits more complex tasks that rely heavily on single-core performance.

Multi-core performance has also seen substantial improvements. The M4 chip excels at handling parallel tasks, making it ideal for activities like video editing, 3D rendering, and running complex simulations. This is particularly evident in the M4 Pro variant of the Mac Mini, which is tailored for professional users who require even more computational power without sacrificing the compact form factor.

The advancements in the M4 chip aren't limited to raw processing power. Apple has also made significant strides in machine learning capabilities. The enhanced neural engine accelerates tasks involving artificial intelligence and machine learning, such as image recognition and natural language processing. This not only improves current applications but also opens the door for more advanced software that can leverage these capabilities in the future.

Efficiency remains a cornerstone of the M4 chip's design. Despite the increases in performance, the chip maintains low power consumption and heat generation. This balance is crucial for the Mac Mini's small enclosure, which doesn't have the space for extensive cooling systems found in larger desktops. The result is a machine that runs quietly and stays cool under pressure, all while delivering top-tier performance.

Comparing the M4 chip to the M1 and M2 generations highlights the rapid pace of innovation in Apple's silicon development. Each iteration has brought significant improvements, but the M4 represents a more substantial leap forward. It's not just an incremental upgrade; it's a reimagining of what Apple's chips can achieve. This progress underscores Apple's advantage in designing both the hardware and software for its devices, allowing for optimizations that competitors find hard to match.

In summary, the M4 chip is a game-changer that propels the Mac Mini into a new realm of capability. It combines high-performance computing with energy efficiency in a way that complements the Mac Mini's compact design. For users, this means access to a powerful desktop experience that was previously unattainable in such a small package. The M4 chip doesn't just keep pace with the demands of modern computing—it sets a new standard for what can be expected from a compact desktop machine.

The M4 chip in the latest Mac Mini is a marvel of modern engineering, delivering performance that feels almost too good to be true for a machine of its size and price point. Built on Apple's refined silicon architecture, it excels in handling a broad range of tasks with seamless efficiency, from everyday multitasking to medium-grade professional workloads and even light creative projects. Its power, paired with its diminutive form factor, redefines expectations for compact computing.

For day-to-day activities, the M4 Mac Mini is a powerhouse. Browsing the web, streaming music or video, managing multiple tabs in Arc or Safari, and juggling apps all happen without a hiccup. Even when pushed with demanding multitasking scenarios, like running virtual machines or working with large datasets in productivity tools, the M4 chip maintains its responsiveness. This level of performance ensures that users who rely on their computers for work or play can do so without ever feeling constrained by the hardware.

The M4 Mac Mini also caters well to medium-grade professional tasks. Photo editing in tools like Pixelmator or Adobe Lightroom runs smoothly, with no lag when applying adjustments or exporting high-resolution images. Coding environments thrive on the M4, as its fast single-core performance is ideal for compiling code or running lightweight development servers. It handles video editing at a moderate level too, making it a solid choice for creators who don't need ultra-high-end hardware but still want a machine capable of managing their workflows efficiently.

One of the unsung heroes of the M4 Mac Mini's performance is its cooling design. Apple has re-engineered the thermal management system to accommodate the chip's impressive capabilities without compromising the compact dimensions. The M4 Mac Mini features a single, intelligently designed fan that rarely needs to ramp up to audible levels, even under load. When it does, the sound is barely noticeable, and the system quickly returns to its usual quiet operation. This efficient thermal management not only prevents throttling during intensive tasks but also extends the longevity of the hardware by keeping it at optimal operating temperatures.

The standout feature of the M4 chip, however, is its single-core performance. Apple has set a new standard with the M4, achieving record-breaking speeds in this category. Single-core performance is a critical metric for many everyday tasks, as it determines how quickly and efficiently the system can process individual instructions. This is particularly important for applications that are not heavily multi-threaded, such as web browsing, certain productivity apps, and even elements of creative workflows.

The M4's dominance in single-core performance is no accident. Apple's mastery of both hardware and software allows the chip to leverage every ounce of its potential, working in harmony with macOS to deliver lightning-fast responsiveness. Benchmarks confirm that the M4 chip surpasses not only its predecessors but also many competing processors in this regard, making it the fastest single-core performer in Apple's entire lineup.

This exceptional single-core speed doesn't just translate into faster app launches or quicker file handling—it defines the experience of using the M4 Mac Mini. Every interaction feels immediate, every task effortless, creating a level of fluidity that's difficult to describe but impossible to ignore. Combined with its efficient multi-core performance, the M4 chip strikes a balance that makes the Mac

Mini a versatile tool for a wide range of users. It's not just about raw power; it's about how that power translates into real-world usability, solidifying the M4 Mac Mini as a leader in its class.

Chapter 4: The Base Model Advantage

The M4 Mac Mini base model, priced at $599, is being celebrated as one of the best deals in technology today—and for good reason. In a world where high-performance computing often comes with a hefty price tag, this compact desktop delivers exceptional value, offering cutting-edge features at a cost that feels almost too good to be true.

At the heart of this deal is Apple's decision to double the unified memory in the base model to 16GB, a substantial upgrade over previous generations. Unified memory, which is shared seamlessly between the CPU, GPU, and Neural Engine, is a cornerstone of Apple's silicon architecture. This enhancement allows the M4 Mac Mini to handle demanding multitasking scenarios effortlessly, from running multiple browser tabs to juggling productivity apps, without any noticeable slowdown.

The inclusion of the M4 chip in the base configuration is another standout feature. This processor, with its 10-core CPU and 10-core GPU, offers an impressive balance of performance and efficiency. It's capable of powering through everyday tasks with ease while also managing medium-grade professional workloads, such as photo editing and light coding. The M4 chip's energy efficiency ensures that users get the best of both worlds: robust performance and low power consumption.

Storage in the base model comes in at 256GB, which is sufficient for many users who rely on cloud storage or external drives for larger files. While it may not seem like much for those handling significant amounts of media, it's a sensible inclusion for an entry-level device, allowing Apple to keep the price accessible. Additionally, the blazing-fast SSD ensures quick boot times, snappy app launches, and smooth overall performance, even with the limited capacity.

What truly sets the $599 Mac Mini apart is its ability to deliver this level of performance and hardware in a device of its size. Competing products in the same price range often compromise on build quality, performance, or long-term value, but the M4 Mac Mini strikes a remarkable balance. It's a perfect entry point for users new to macOS, students on a budget, or professionals looking for a secondary machine.

The affordability of the base model doesn't just make it accessible—it positions the M4 Mac Mini as a gateway into Apple's ecosystem. For users seeking the power of macOS and the efficiency of Apple silicon without the premium price of an iMac or MacBook, this desktop offers an unbeatable combination of value and capability. The $599 price tag isn't just a good deal; it's a statement, proving that high-performance computing can be both accessible and uncompromising.

When placed alongside the M4 iMac and Mac Studio, the M4 Mac Mini stands out not only for its compactness but also for its remarkable balance of performance and affordability. Each of these machines caters to a distinct audience, but the Mac Mini carves a unique niche by delivering power and flexibility in a device that's both portable and budget-friendly.

The M4 iMac, while visually stunning with its vibrant display and integrated design, starts at $1,299—more than double the price of the base Mac Mini. Functionally, the two machines share the same M4 chip in their base configurations, offering nearly identical processing power. However, the iMac includes a 24-inch Retina display, which accounts for much of the price difference. For those who already own a monitor or prefer the flexibility of choosing their display, the Mac Mini's $700 savings becomes an obvious advantage. It allows users to pair the Mac Mini with a display that suits their specific needs and preferences, rather than being tied to the iMac's built-in screen.

Comparisons with the Mac Studio further emphasize the Mac Mini's appeal as an efficient and affordable powerhouse. The Mac Studio, designed for high-end professional workflows, starts at $1,999 and is equipped with Apple's more advanced M2 Max or Ultra chips. While it offers unparalleled performance for intensive tasks like 3D rendering and large-scale video production, this level of power is far beyond what most users need. For those whose workloads fall within the range of the M4 chip's capabilities, the Mac Mini provides a cost-effective alternative without the excess power—and cost—of the Mac Studio.

Storage and memory limitations do play a role in how the Mac Mini compares to its larger siblings. The base model comes with 256GB of storage, which is significantly less than the options available on the iMac or Mac Studio. For users handling large media files, such as high-resolution videos or extensive photo libraries, this limitation may require an investment in external storage solutions or an upgrade at the time of purchase. However, for general users relying on cloud storage or external drives, the base storage can be sufficient without impacting productivity.

The 16GB of unified memory in the base model is a standout feature, ensuring smooth multitasking and efficient performance for most applications. While higher memory configurations are available on the Mac Studio, the base memory on the Mac Mini is ample for tasks like browsing, photo editing, and light coding. However, users working with highly demanding software or multitasking at a professional level may benefit from the Mac Studio's expanded memory options.

Ultimately, the M4 Mac Mini thrives in its role as a versatile and affordable option within Apple's lineup. It may lack the integrated display of the iMac or the extreme power of the Mac Studio, but it compensates with unmatched flexibility and value. By offering high performance in a compact form factor, the Mac Mini caters to a wide range of users, from casual consumers to professionals, proving that sometimes less really is more.

Chapter 5: Understanding Apple's Upgrade Strategy

Apple has mastered the art of the "price ladder," a strategy designed to guide users toward higher-cost configurations by presenting incremental upgrades that seem too tempting to pass up. The M4 Mac Mini exemplifies this approach, with a base model that offers outstanding value but also invites users to consider spending more for enhanced features. It's a clever tactic that makes upgrading feel almost inevitable, yet it can significantly impact the affordability of what begins as a budget-friendly machine.

The base M4 Mac Mini starts at $599, an undeniably attractive price for a machine with such powerful hardware. However, it's configured with 256GB of storage, a limitation that may prompt many users to explore upgrades. For example, doubling the storage to 512GB costs an additional $200, and upgrading to a full terabyte requires a $400 investment. Suddenly, the compact and affordable Mac Mini begins to edge closer to the price of higher-tier products in Apple's lineup.

Beyond storage, Apple offers other upgrade options that add to the allure of moving up the price ladder. Increasing the unified memory from 16GB to 32GB costs $400, a significant leap but one that might appeal to professionals running memory-intensive applications. Similarly, upgrading the Ethernet port from standard Gigabit to 10 Gigabit Ethernet adds $100, a feature most casual users may not need but one that could prove irresistible to those seeking advanced networking capabilities.

These incremental costs are not unique to the Mac Mini; they are a cornerstone of Apple's pricing strategy across its product lines. By making each upgrade feel like a logical step up in value, Apple encourages users to customize their devices in ways that ultimately increase the final price. The psychological impact is subtle yet effective—what begins as a $599 purchase can quickly escalate into a $1,200 investment once storage, memory, and other upgrades are factored in.

The key to understanding Apple's price ladder is recognizing how it plays on user needs and aspirations. For instance, a user might justify spending an additional $200 on storage, thinking of it as a long-term investment. Once that decision is made, the leap to more memory or faster Ethernet might feel like a natural extension of that logic. Before they know it, the user has climbed several rungs of the price ladder, often spending far more than initially intended.

While this strategy undeniably boosts Apple's profitability, it also raises questions about value. The base model of the M4 Mac Mini is a fantastic deal on its own, but for users tempted by multiple upgrades, the price begins to approach that of higher-tier devices like the iMac or even the Mac Studio. At some point, the line between upgrading a Mac Mini and purchasing a more powerful system starts to blur, leaving buyers to weigh the trade-offs carefully.

For those considering the M4 Mac Mini, the best approach is to assess their needs realistically before succumbing to the allure of upgrades. By understanding Apple's pricing strategy and resisting the pull of the price ladder, users can maximize the value of their purchase while keeping costs under control. After all, the true genius of the M4 Mac Mini lies in its ability to deliver high performance at an accessible price—a promise that only holds if the buyer stays mindful of the incremental costs along the way.

Deciding whether to upgrade the M4 Mac Mini beyond its base model comes down to understanding your specific needs and balancing them against the costs. Apple's upgrade options can add significant capability to the machine, but they also come with steep price tags that may not always represent the best value. Knowing when an upgrade is truly necessary can help users make informed choices without overpaying for features they might not fully utilize.

For general users—those focused on web browsing, streaming, light productivity tasks, and occasional photo editing—the base M4 Mac Mini is more than adequate. With its 16GB of unified memory, 256GB of storage, and the M4 chip's outstanding single-core performance, it handles everyday multitasking with ease. These users likely won't need to climb the upgrade ladder unless they anticipate growing storage demands or have a specific requirement for faster networking.

However, some scenarios do justify spending more. Creative professionals who regularly work with large media files—such as high-resolution images, videos, or music production—may benefit from additional storage or memory. Video editors, for instance, might find the 256GB base storage limiting, as large video projects can quickly fill the drive. Upgrading to 512GB or even 1TB can ensure a smoother workflow without the constant need for external drives. Similarly, professionals running memory-intensive software like virtual machines or large databases might find the 16GB base memory insufficient, making the jump to 32GB worthwhile.

Another category of users who might consider upgrading is those in fields requiring high-speed networking. The optional 10 Gigabit Ethernet upgrade is a game-changer for users working with large datasets over a network, such as video editors accessing shared storage or IT professionals managing server environments. For these specific cases, the additional $100 for faster networking might be a justifiable investment.

Despite these valid use cases, it's important to remain cautious about Apple's upgrade pricing. The costs escalate quickly, often leading to diminishing returns. For example, upgrading from the base 256GB storage to 1TB adds $400—nearly as much as the price of a second base model Mac Mini. Similarly, boosting memory to 32GB adds another $400, which might make users question whether the extra capability is worth doubling the machine's price.

The pitfalls of Apple's pricing structure also lie in the lack of flexibility post-purchase. Storage and memory upgrades must be made at the time of purchase, as these components are soldered directly to the motherboard. This forces buyers to anticipate their future needs upfront, often leading to overpaying "just in case." While Apple's upgrade pricing ensures premium components and seamless integration, it doesn't offer much leeway for users who might want to scale up gradually.

For users tempted to climb the upgrade ladder, external solutions like USB-C or Thunderbolt-connected storage can provide a more cost-effective alternative. Similarly, evaluating whether the added expense of upgrades could instead be allocated toward a higher-tier device, such as the Mac Studio, is another strategy to ensure the best value for your investment.

Ultimately, the decision to upgrade hinges on understanding your current and future needs. While the M4 Mac Mini's base model is an exceptional deal, its upgrade options cater to specific use cases that may or may not apply to every buyer. By carefully weighing the benefits of each upgrade against the steep costs, users can make smarter purchasing decisions that align with both their needs and their budgets.

Chapter 6: The Pro-Level Performer

The M4 Pro Mac Mini is a compelling choice for users who demand more from their desktop. Positioned between the base Mac Mini and Apple's higher-end offerings like the Mac Studio, this model is designed for creative professionals, developers, and power users who need performance without compromising on portability or affordability. It's an ideal solution for those who require the capabilities of a high-end machine but in a form factor that's easy to integrate into diverse workflows, whether at home, in the office, or on the go.

One of the standout qualities of the M4 Pro Mac Mini is its suitability as a portable workstation. For professionals like video editors, graphic designers, and music producers, the M4 Pro provides a significant performance boost over the base model while maintaining the compact design that defines the Mac Mini line. Equipped with the M4 Pro chip, this machine offers additional CPU and GPU cores, enabling it to handle complex tasks like 4K video editing, 3D modeling, and audio mixing with ease. Its enhanced processing power ensures smoother rendering times, faster exports, and the ability to manage larger projects without the bottlenecks often encountered on less capable machines.

Portability is another key factor that makes the M4 Pro Mac Mini stand out for creative professionals. Unlike the Mac Studio or iMac, which are designed to remain stationary, the Mac Mini's small footprint and lightweight design make it easy to transport. Whether you're moving between studios, working on-location shoots, or simply needing to relocate your setup, the M4 Pro fits effortlessly into a travel bag or Pelican case. For those accustomed to lugging heavier, bulkier equipment, this machine represents a liberating shift toward efficiency and flexibility.

The M4 Pro Mac Mini also supports a wide range of peripherals, making it a versatile hub for professional workflows. With upgraded Thunderbolt 5 ports, it can handle up to three 6K displays simultaneously, a feature that's invaluable for video editors and digital artists who rely on multiple screens for their work. These ports also allow for high-speed data transfer, enabling seamless connections to external drives, professional-grade audio interfaces, and other essential tools.

Moreover, its memory and storage configurations cater to demanding tasks. The M4 Pro model offers up to 48GB of unified memory, providing ample headroom for multitasking across intensive applications. This is particularly useful for workflows involving virtual machines, large-scale image editing, or complex coding projects. While storage upgrades come at a premium, the ability to configure the Mac Mini with up to 8TB of SSD space ensures that even the most data-heavy projects can be managed locally without reliance on external storage solutions.

What truly sets the M4 Pro Mac Mini apart is its balance of performance and cost-effectiveness. An equivalent MacBook Pro with the M4 Pro chip starts at $2,000, making the $1,399 price point of the M4 Pro Mac Mini an attractive alternative for those who don't require a built-in display or portability in a laptop format. For professionals who already have a preferred monitor or work in setups with multiple screens, the Mac Mini provides a streamlined, plug-and-play experience that maximizes value.

Ultimately, the M4 Pro Mac Mini is for those who need more than what the base model offers but don't require the extreme power—or price—of the Mac Studio. It's a workstation for creatives and power users who value performance, adaptability, and portability in equal measure. By delivering professional-grade capabilities in a machine small enough to fit in your hand, the M4 Pro Mac Mini exemplifies Apple's ability to redefine what a desktop computer can be.

The M4 Pro chip represents a significant leap forward in Apple's silicon lineup, offering enhanced capabilities tailored for professionals who need a balance of power and efficiency. Building on the architecture of the base M4 chip, the Pro version delivers additional CPU and GPU cores, expanded memory bandwidth, and advanced features that make it a standout option for demanding workflows. It's not just a step up—it's a tool designed to handle complex, resource-intensive tasks with ease, redefining what's possible in a compact desktop computer.

At the core of the M4 Pro chip is a 12-core CPU, which features a mix of high-performance and efficiency cores. This configuration allows the chip to manage heavy workloads like video editing, 3D rendering, and compiling code while maintaining energy efficiency for lighter tasks. The GPU, now boasting up to 16 cores, provides a substantial boost for graphics-intensive applications, making it ideal for professionals working in motion graphics, gaming, or augmented reality development. Combined with an upgraded Neural Engine for machine learning tasks, the M4 Pro chip is a powerhouse capable of handling the most demanding creative and computational workflows.

Real-world performance benchmarks highlight the chip's capabilities. In single-core tasks, the M4 Pro continues to lead the industry with unmatched responsiveness, ensuring that even everyday operations feel fast and fluid. Its multi-core performance, meanwhile, places it among the best in Apple's lineup, with synthetic benchmarks revealing a noticeable improvement over the base M4 chip and even rivaling the M2 Max in specific scenarios. GPU benchmarks show the M4 Pro delivering performance equivalent to the M1 Max, underscoring the generational progress Apple has achieved with its silicon.

In practical terms, this performance translates to faster rendering times, smoother playback of high-resolution video, and the ability to work on large projects without lag or interruptions. For professionals working in creative fields, the M4 Pro chip eliminates many of the bottlenecks associated with less capable machines. Whether you're editing 8K footage, running simulations, or working with large datasets, the M4 Pro delivers the performance needed to get the job done efficiently.

When compared to other high-end Macs, the M4 Pro Mac Mini stands out for its cost-to-performance ratio. A similarly configured MacBook Pro with the M4 Pro chip starts at $2,000, offering portability and an integrated display but at a significantly higher price. For users who don't require a laptop or already have a preferred monitor setup, the Mac Mini provides equivalent performance in a more affordable package. Its $1,399 starting price makes it an appealing choice for budget-conscious professionals who prioritize desktop power over portability.

The Mac Studio, on the other hand, offers even greater performance with options for the M2 Max or M2 Ultra chips. However, this comes at a premium, with prices starting at $1,999 and climbing steeply for higher configurations. While the Mac Studio is better suited for extreme workloads, many users will find the M4 Pro Mac Mini more than sufficient for their needs, particularly if their tasks don't demand the additional GPU power or memory bandwidth of the Mac Studio.

Portability is another factor where the M4 Pro Mac Mini excels. Unlike the Mac Studio or iMac, the Mac Mini's compact design makes it easy to transport between locations, whether for remote work, studio sessions, or on-site presentations. It offers a unique combination of desktop-level power and mobility that's unmatched by other machines in its class.

In terms of trade-offs, the M4 Pro Mac Mini's primary limitation is its reliance on external peripherals. Unlike the MacBook Pro or iMac, it doesn't include a built-in display, keyboard, or trackpad. While this adds flexibility in customizing a workspace, it also means additional expenses for those starting from scratch. Additionally, Apple's premium pricing for upgrades—such as increased storage or memory—can quickly erode its cost advantage, making it essential for users to carefully evaluate their needs before committing to configurations.

Overall, the M4 Pro Mac Mini strikes an impressive balance between cost, performance, and portability. It offers professional-grade power in a compact form factor at a price that undercuts many of Apple's high-end options. For creative professionals, developers, and power users seeking a workstation that doesn't compromise on performance or budget, the M4 Pro Mac Mini is a compelling choice that embodies Apple's vision of the future of computing.

Chapter 7: Breaking Down the Competition

The M4 Mac Mini enters a competitive landscape in the world of compact PCs, where custom mini ITX builds and small desktop systems have long been the go-to options for enthusiasts and professionals seeking power in a small form factor. While these alternatives offer flexibility and performance, the M4 Mac Mini distinguishes itself with a combination of engineering, efficiency, and seamless integration that is difficult for competitors to match.

Custom mini ITX builds have traditionally been the gold standard for compact PCs, allowing users to tailor their systems to specific needs. Enthusiasts often assemble these builds with carefully selected components, such as high-performance CPUs, discrete GPUs, and customizable storage and memory options. While this approach offers unmatched versatility, it also requires significant expertise and effort. Building a mini ITX system involves considerations like thermal management, power supply constraints, and compatibility between components, making it less accessible for casual users.

By contrast, the M4 Mac Mini provides an all-in-one solution that eliminates the complexity of custom builds. Its compact 5x5x2-inch design houses a powerful M4 chip, which integrates CPU, GPU, and memory in a unified architecture, maximizing efficiency while minimizing physical space requirements. Unlike mini ITX systems that rely on separate components, the M4 Mac Mini's tightly integrated design ensures optimal performance with minimal heat output and noise, all without the need for user intervention.

When it comes to other pre-built small desktops, such as Intel NUCs or specialized gaming PCs like those from Zotac or ASUS, the M4 Mac Mini holds its own. Many of these systems boast impressive hardware configurations, including discrete graphics cards and high-wattage CPUs, making them suitable for gaming or highly intensive tasks. However, these machines often sacrifice energy efficiency and compactness for raw power, resulting in larger footprints, louder fans, and higher electricity consumption.

The M4 Mac Mini's energy efficiency sets it apart in this regard. Thanks to the advanced 3-nanometer process used in the M4 chip, it delivers industry-leading performance per watt. This makes it an excellent choice for users who prioritize sustainability or need a quiet machine for their workspace. Additionally, its thermal design allows it to operate almost silently under most conditions, a feature that many competitors struggle to achieve in such a compact form factor.

In terms of pricing, the M4 Mac Mini's $599 starting point positions it as a strong value proposition in the compact PC market. Custom mini ITX builds can easily exceed this price once high-quality components and assembly costs are factored in, while pre-built systems often start at similar or higher price points without offering the same level of integration or macOS's optimized software experience. For users who value simplicity and out-of-the-box functionality, the Mac Mini offers a compelling alternative to these options.

One area where competitors do have an advantage is in upgradability. Custom mini ITX builds and many small desktops allow users to swap out components over time, such as upgrading the GPU, adding more RAM, or increasing storage capacity. The M4 Mac Mini, on the other hand, features soldered memory and storage, meaning upgrades must be selected at the time of purchase. While this approach enhances efficiency and reduces size, it may deter users who prefer the flexibility of modular systems.

Despite this limitation, the M4 Mac Mini excels in delivering a user experience that's hard to replicate with other compact PCs. Its seamless integration of hardware and software, combined with its elegant design and unmatched energy efficiency, makes it a standout choice for professionals, creatives, and general users alike. For those seeking a powerful yet hassle-free compact desktop, the M4 Mac Mini proves that great things truly can come in small packages.

Apple Silicon has redefined the computing landscape, and the M4 Mac Mini exemplifies why it stands unmatched in the realm of compact desktops. By leveraging its in-house chip design, Apple has achieved a level of integration, efficiency, and performance that competitors struggle to replicate. The M4 Mac Mini is a masterclass in balance, delivering power and portability without compromise—something no other compact desktop currently matches.

At the heart of this achievement is the M4 chip, built on Apple's unified architecture. Unlike traditional systems that rely on separate CPU, GPU, and memory components, Apple Silicon combines these elements into a single chip. This integration minimizes latency, enhances communication between components, and allows for unparalleled efficiency. The result is a machine that performs like a high-end desktop while maintaining an energy footprint closer to that of a laptop.

Size is another area where the M4 Mac Mini leads. Measuring just five inches by five inches and two inches tall, it is significantly smaller than most compact desktops, including custom mini ITX builds or other pre-built systems. Achieving this level of miniaturization without sacrificing performance is a testament to Apple's meticulous engineering. Competitors often face trade-offs, sacrificing size for performance or vice versa, but the M4 Mac Mini proves that you can have both.

Efficiency is another cornerstone of Apple Silicon's advantage. Thanks to the M4 chip's advanced 3-nanometer manufacturing process, the Mac Mini delivers industry-leading performance per watt. This efficiency translates to quieter operation, less heat output, and lower energy consumption—ideal for users seeking a powerful yet sustainable computing solution. Many compact desktops with similar performance levels rely on power-hungry components, requiring larger cooling systems that increase noise and size. The M4 Mac Mini's near-silent operation and cool temperatures set it apart in this regard.

The synergy between Apple's hardware and software further solidifies its advantage. MacOS is specifically optimized for Apple Silicon, ensuring that the M4 Mac Mini's hardware is used to its fullest potential. Tasks like app launches, multitasking, and file transfers feel instantaneous, a level of responsiveness that competing systems often can't match due to the fragmented nature of their hardware and software ecosystems. This seamless integration also ensures long-term reliability and updates that maintain the machine's relevance for years.

While competitors in the compact PC space offer certain advantages, such as upgradability or specific hardware configurations, they often lack the all-encompassing balance of the M4 Mac Mini. Custom mini ITX builds may provide powerful GPUs or modular flexibility, but they require careful planning, can be noisy, and rarely achieve the same level of energy efficiency. Similarly, pre-built systems like Intel NUCs or gaming mini PCs excel in certain niches but often fall short in size or integration.

Apple's holistic approach allows the M4 Mac Mini to outshine these alternatives. It isn't just a collection of impressive specifications—it's a cohesive system where every element works in harmony to deliver an unparalleled user experience. The combination of power, efficiency, and compactness makes it a game-changer for professionals, creatives, and everyday users alike. The M4 Mac Mini is a bold statement that computing doesn't need to be a choice between performance and practicality—it can be both.

Chapter 8: The Future of Compact Computing

The M4 Mac Mini holds a distinctive and strategic place in Apple's product lineup, underscoring the company's commitment to compact yet powerful computing. Over the years, the Mac Mini has evolved from being a niche product to becoming a cornerstone of Apple's vision for accessible, versatile desktops. With the release of the M4 version, it cements its role as a key entry point into the macOS ecosystem while pushing the boundaries of what compact desktops can achieve.

In Apple's broader strategy, the Mac Mini serves as a bridge between affordability and performance. It offers users the opportunity to experience the power of Apple Silicon without the higher price tags associated with the iMac or Mac Studio. This positioning makes it a critical component of Apple's portfolio, appealing to a wide audience, from casual users to professionals seeking a secondary machine or a portable workstation. For developers, creative professionals, and educators, the Mac Mini provides an affordable yet capable platform, ensuring that macOS remains accessible to a diverse range of users.

The introduction of the M4 Mac Mini also signals Apple's focus on refining its products rather than overhauling them. By maintaining the essence of the Mac Mini—its compact design and affordability—while incorporating significant advancements in performance and efficiency, Apple demonstrates its ability to innovate within established frameworks. This iterative approach ensures that the Mac Mini stays relevant without alienating its core audience, a balance that is crucial in a competitive market.

Looking ahead, the M4 Mac Mini could pave the way for exciting future developments in compact computing. As Apple continues to advance its silicon technology, we can expect even greater performance gains in subsequent generations. The transition from the M1 to the M4 has already demonstrated Apple's ability to deliver exponential improvements in power and efficiency, and the roadmap for future chips promises to continue this trend.

Speculations about the future of the Mac Mini also include potential design changes and expanded capabilities. While the M4 version represents a significant reduction in size, future iterations may explore even more compact or modular designs, catering to users who value flexibility and portability. Innovations in cooling technology and power management could allow for even more powerful configurations without increasing the machine's physical footprint or noise levels.

On the software side, the Mac Mini's role could expand further as macOS continues to integrate features that enhance productivity and creativity. With growing trends in remote work, education, and creative industries, the Mac Mini could see additional features that cater to these evolving needs, such as improved collaboration tools,

AI-driven optimizations, and enhanced compatibility with external peripherals.

The Mac Mini also hints at a broader trend in the computing industry: the rise of compact, energy-efficient devices that don't compromise on performance. As consumer priorities shift toward sustainability and minimalism, the demand for devices like the Mac Mini is likely to grow. Apple is well-positioned to lead this trend, using its expertise in silicon and hardware design to redefine what users expect from desktop computers.

In the long term, the M4 Mac Mini's success could influence the development of Apple's other product lines. Its emphasis on portability, power, and price accessibility could inspire similar approaches in future updates to the iMac, Mac Studio, or even the Mac Pro. By offering a compelling combination of features at an attractive price point, the Mac Mini ensures that Apple remains competitive across all segments of the desktop market.

The M4 Mac Mini isn't just another product—it's a statement about Apple's vision for the future of computing. Its role as a compact, versatile, and affordable machine reinforces Apple's commitment to innovation and accessibility, setting the stage for what's to come in the world of desktop technology.

Apple's design philosophy, as showcased by the M4 Mac Mini, is fundamentally reshaping how we think about desktop computers. Traditionally, desktops were synonymous with large, bulky towers that prioritized raw power over portability or elegance. Apple, however, has consistently challenged this notion, crafting machines that balance performance, efficiency, and aesthetic simplicity. With the M4 Mac Mini, Apple has redefined compact computing, proving that size is no longer a barrier to power.

The M4 Mac Mini exemplifies Apple's vision of delivering "compact power for all." By harnessing the efficiency of the M4 chip, Apple has managed to condense high-performance computing into a device that is smaller than many everyday objects. Its 5x5x2-inch footprint is a testament to the company's ability to innovate without compromise, offering a level of capability that rivals larger desktops while maintaining a sleek and unobtrusive design. This approach challenges the long-standing perception that powerful desktops must dominate workspace real estate.

One of the key elements of Apple's design philosophy is its focus on integration. The M4 Mac Mini embodies this principle with its unified architecture, where the CPU, GPU, and memory work seamlessly together. This integration not only optimizes performance but also reduces the machine's physical requirements, enabling Apple to shrink its size without sacrificing functionality. It's a design that prioritizes user experience, ensuring that every inch of the Mac Mini serves a purpose.

This compact power extends beyond performance to include energy efficiency and quiet operation. The M4 chip's 3-nanometer process allows it to deliver exceptional performance per watt, making the M4 Mac Mini one of the most energy-efficient desktops available. Its advanced cooling system, featuring a single quiet fan, ensures that even under heavy workloads, the device remains nearly silent. These features align with modern consumer values, where sustainability and convenience are increasingly prioritized alongside raw power.

Apple's design philosophy also emphasizes accessibility, and the M4 Mac Mini is a shining example of this commitment. Its affordability—starting at $599—makes it a gateway into macOS for a wide range of users. Students, educators, developers, and creative professionals can all benefit from its power without the prohibitive costs associated with high-end desktops. This democratization of performance ensures that advanced computing isn't limited to those with large budgets, fostering inclusivity in the tech world.

Moreover, the M4 Mac Mini challenges other manufacturers to rethink their approach to compact desktops. Competing systems often require trade-offs, such as limited upgradeability, noisy cooling, or reduced performance to achieve smaller sizes. Apple's holistic approach—combining powerful hardware, efficient design, and seamless software integration—sets a new standard for what compact desktops can and should be. It encourages the industry to prioritize not just smaller devices but smarter ones that enhance the user experience in meaningful ways.

The impact of Apple's design philosophy extends beyond the Mac Mini itself. By redefining the desktop form factor, Apple is shaping broader consumer expectations. Users now seek devices that are not only powerful but also versatile, energy-efficient, and aesthetically pleasing. This shift influences trends across the tech industry, from home offices to creative studios, as companies strive to meet the elevated standards Apple has set.

The M4 Mac Mini is more than just a product—it's a manifestation of Apple's vision for the future of computing. Its design philosophy challenges the status quo, proving that desktops can be compact, powerful, and accessible to all. In doing so, Apple is reshaping what users expect from their machines, driving innovation that will undoubtedly inspire the next generation of computing devices.

Conclusion

The M4 Mac Mini is a game-changer in the world of compact desktops, embodying Apple's vision for the future of computing. It matters not just for what it is—a remarkably small, powerful, and energy-efficient machine—but for what it represents: a redefinition of how performance, design, and accessibility can coexist. By leveraging the power of the M4 chip and Apple's unified architecture, the M4 Mac Mini has set a new standard for what users can expect from a desktop computer, reshaping the industry in the process.

Its impact on the tech world is significant. The M4 Mac Mini showcases the potential of Apple Silicon, proving that size no longer dictates performance. It pushes the boundaries of what compact computing can achieve, challenging competitors to rethink their designs and innovations. In an era where sustainability, efficiency, and minimalism are increasingly valued, the M4 Mac Mini emerges as a leader, demonstrating that high performance and responsible design can go hand in hand.

This device also highlights Apple's unique ability to integrate hardware and software seamlessly. The optimization between the M4 chip and macOS ensures a level of responsiveness and fluidity that is difficult to replicate with competing systems. It's not just about raw specifications; it's about how those specs translate into real-world usability, creating a desktop that feels both powerful and effortless.

The M4 Mac Mini's appeal extends to a wide range of users. For casual users, it's an affordable entry point into the macOS ecosystem, offering unmatched value at $599. Students, educators, and budget-conscious consumers will find it an excellent choice for everyday tasks like web browsing, streaming, and productivity. For creative professionals and developers, the M4 Pro version delivers the additional power needed for more demanding workflows, all while maintaining portability and affordability.

Businesses and IT professionals can also benefit from the M4 Mac Mini's compact design and energy efficiency, making it an ideal solution for space-constrained environments or large-scale deployments. Its quiet operation and robust performance make it equally suitable for offices, studios, and home setups.

Ultimately, the M4 Mac Mini is a testament to Apple's ability to innovate within established frameworks. It serves as a reminder that great design isn't about making something smaller or faster alone—it's about creating a device that integrates seamlessly into the lives of its users, delivering power and simplicity in equal measure. Whether you're a first-time Mac user or a seasoned professional, the M4 Mac Mini offers something extraordinary: a desktop that redefines what's possible, inspiring us to rethink the role of technology in our daily lives.

www.ingramcontent.com/pod-product-compliance
Lightning Source LLC
LaVergne TN
LVHW052321060326
832902LV00023B/4518